T0146723

INSTANT OBEDIENCE

LAUREL DURHAM-JOHN

authorHOUSE®

AuthorHouse™
1663 Liberty Drive
Bloomington, IN 47403
www.authorhouse.com
Phone: 1 (800) 839-8640

Published by AuthorHouse 09/08/2016

ISBN: 978-1-5246-2756-0 (sc)
ISBN: 978-1-5246-2755-3 (e)

Library of Congress Control Number: 2016914432

Print information available on the last page.

Contents

Dedication

This book is dedicated to my daughter. You are a huge part of the reason why I persevere. You can achieve my darling, don't ever give up.

Acknowledgements

First and foremost thanks to God for His unconditional love, without it I would not be here.

Thanks to my daughter for helping me to persevere. You have been a light in my life.

Thanks to my parents James J and Veltie Durham for your words of wisdom, love, inspiration and prayers. You have been there for me throughout the years.

Thanks to Mineva Glasgow, Dawn Joseph, and Nema Henry and the all others who were instrumental in the production of this book.

Thanks to Gloria Farrell, Velma Samuel, Natasha James, Pastor Howard and Michelle Simon and others who have prayed for me.

Chapter 1 On Angels Wings

ℑ was about eight months pregnant when my husband and I had gone to visit my parents one evening. It was approximately a six-mile drive and the evening was cool. We arrived at my parents' house around dusk, that time of the day when the fireflies and bats start flying about, coming out of their sleeping positions. On entering my parents' house, we

This reflection reminds me of the text Psalm 91: 11-12, "For He shall give his angels charge over thee to keep thee in all thy ways. They shall bear thee up in their hands, lest thou dash thy foot against a stone." My friends trust Jesus, call on Him. He keeps His promises.

headed towards the living room where we chatted and laughed.

𝕴 left the room to get something and upon my return, while standing in the doorway, I saw a creature flying towards me from the far end of the living room. It was a bat. I was scared out of my wits. My first instinct was to run and I started running to get out of the way. Then I tripped and was falling. I was falling onto my very big eight months stomach. I cried out to the Lord within my heart. I said, "Jesus, **what is this?** Have I reached this far only to lose everything now?" Such pain was within me. Then I heard a voice say, "Hold on to the backrest of the easy chair in front of you." While falling, I stretched my hands towards the backrest of the chair to get a hold of it. Suddenly, I heard a loud noise. It was the sound of someone who fell and hit the floor, but, I did not feel it.

I felt myself being gently rested onto the floor on my knees. It felt as if an angel took the blow that was intended for me and gently rested me unto my knees. Amazingly, my knees were not bruised, my stomach with my eight-month baby did not jolt, it should have because of the loud noise that was heard, but it did not. No bruises. Nothing at all.

My husband and mom looked at me in awe. What had they just witnessed? My husband said he heard the noise too. To this day, all I can say is that my Jesus saved me from falling onto my eight-month pregnant stomach, showing me even in a split second when the tragedy was about to strike, He was right there to help.

Chapter 2   Proving God

In the earlier stages of our marriage, my spouse and I were on one of our Sunday afternoon get together with our friends. On this particular afternoon we headed to the beach. It had rained heavily the day and night before, and a little stream which runs into that particular bay was muddy, causing the sea to be muddy also. The games began. We were having fun and

There is nothing too small or insignificant for Jesus to handle. He is God. He can handle small things, big things, hurtful things and absolutely anything. Jeremiah 33:3 says, "Call unto me and I will answer thee and shew thee great mighty things which thou knowest not." Be sincere and allow Him to lead.

were into our volleyball game in the water when it happened. I felt it. I felt my wedding rings leaving my fingers while hitting the ball, and I just could not do anything about it. Then they were gone.

I had no idea where they had fallen. I announced to my spouse and friends what had just happened. Just then, I thought of what should I do. I remembered stories my mother read to me as a child, bedtime stories by 'Uncle Arthur', of things being lost and found through prayer. Immediately, I felt deep on the inside, that I must prove God that day, I must prove God. So I asked my spouse and friends to pray. They thought I wanted a group prayer, but no, I wanted to pray within my heart. I wanted each person to do the same also. My reasoning for the personal prayer was I wanted no one to doubt the power of my prayer.

That day I wanted to prove God without anyone questioning or being a hindrance as my prayers ascended to God. The search began. We looked in the area where we figured they may have fallen. We looked for over half an hour but to no avail. The rings could have stayed lost as they were only two small pieces of metal or gold. It was not the rings that were at stake it was my proving God with such a small insignificant matter. We kept looking. I spoke to the Lord again. I said, "Lord, Jesus, it's Sunday evening, it's getting late, we need a miracle. I am going to church this evening, and I don't want to be late."

Soon after, another friend joined us on the beach. He asked us what had happened. We told him. He joined in the search, looking in a different area. Then suddenly, he called my husband and said, "Here are the rings!" Hallelujah! Praise the Lord! My Jesus had come through for me again. The Jesus I heard about in my childhood, from my mom, had come through for me. He had proven Himself.

My husband took a diving mask, went down to the seabed and retrieved the rings. For those who may not have been to the sea, the water is constantly moving, waves coming in and going out. That day the sea water was not clear, it was muddy, but God allowed the glitter of the rings to shine through allowing our friend to see them.

Chapter 3   When I Repented

The music was energizing and the ambiance was enticing. The story happened in my early twenties, while living in Canada. It was the annual independence banquet for my native country. It was an evening in the fall, of lights, friends, food, dress and fashion. I was in attendance. The girls were there, it was dinner and dance. The evening went on in its smooth sensational atmosphere. We ate, laughed, and talked. We simply were having an evening of fun. Then it started, the music was reaching further and further into my soul.

It was not a religious event so you can guess what type of music was playing. As

I sat there dining, the urge came to get up and start enjoying the music in dance. And so, one of my two girlfriends and I got up. We danced and danced to whatever music came on. It felt so good or so I thought. During the dancing I remembered a church sister cautioning us to behave ourselves, but we ignored her and stayed on the dance floor.

Jesus says in Isaiah 1:18; "Come let us reason together saith the Lord, though your sins be as scarlet they shall be white as snow." Even when we are born again, we do mess up and cause God shame. However, He does not leave us there. That only happens if we want to stay there. He stretches out His hand and offers us forgiveness once we asked Him for it. Then there is peace knowing that the Lord has forgiven you.

Then it was time to leave. We left for home and on the way home, the Holy Spirit impressed deeply upon my soul that what I did was wrong. As strongly as the temptation came to dance, as strong was the impression of the Holy Spirit that what I did was wrong, absolutely wrong. I cried and wept bitterly when I realized how much I had just let God down. I repented of my sins before the Lord. Early in the morning, I called my friends and the church sister and repented and asked for forgiveness. While on my way home the night before, I was really troubled and it was only until I gave in to the Master's pleading did I find rest and peace from the act of sin which I committed. It was sweet relief.

Chapter 4 Spared Life

So much was happening at this time. A camp-meeting or some may call it a crusade was about to start. I was preparing for it. The church school where I worked needed some spiritual changes. It seemed as if the behavior of some students were just becoming uncontrollable, more disobedient, and disrespectful. Things were becoming unbearable. My

"With men this is impossible but with God all things are possible." - Matthew 19:26. No matter how dismal a circumstance may look, or how far at the end of the rope you seem to be, remember, it is not the end for you. I am a firm believer that all things are possible with God.

prayer partner, a co-worker, and I continued to pray for changes, for more peace in the school and for students to give honor to God. This was a Christian school. The crusade began and the prayer group, the prayer partners and I, brought the school before the Lord with tears.

Just before the crusade began a new teacher had joined the staff. She asked if I would like to pray with her. She basically said that the Lord is calling her to do something. She looked at the school and realized that there was a need for a greater presence of God. Another teacher also called me on the matter of prayer for the school. We prayed on the phone. The prayer went somewhat like this, "Dear Lord, please let there be a drastic change in what is currently happening in the school, please intervene. We need you desperately." This was on Sunday, Mothers' Day. It seemed as if the Lord was actually speaking to a number of us who were on staff.

The following Monday, the teacher who asked for us to pray together planned that on Thursday of that same week we would start our prayer sessions. However, on Wednesday, it felt as if the enemy was on the loose in the school. At about 2 pm, another co-worker and I had our usual prayer. Just after that prayer, there was a loud banging on the front door of the office. A teacher was banging on the door while shouting, "Call 911!" A student whom she named had fallen over the rails. I proceeded to make the necessary calls and prayed. I called the parents of the child, and the Pastors to pray.

The ambulance came and the chairman of the school board summoned the school with the bullhorn. He asked for everyone to be silent and stay where they were. Then everything stopped and prayer ascended unto heaven for our student. The student who fell from the third floor was unconscious, but came to before leaving in the ambulance. It was an alleged suicide attempt.

The wheels of change had started to turn. Our God is not an advocate for evil. The enemy had meant this for bad, together with the number of things that were happening at the school. However, it is the Lord's school and he worked things together for good for those who love Him at His school. The student survived. Glory to God. The student also recovered to walk and talk as if the incident had not occurred. We had a Jericho prayer walk for the school. The atmosphere changed and there was more peace. God is awesome and tremendous. We thanked God for the spared life of our student. We praised Him over and over again.

Chapter 5   As Small As A
Mustard Seed

When my friend's daughter was only three months old, she contracted a terrible cold that led to bronchitis and eventually asthma. This caused her to have many sleepless nights in and out of the hospital. One Saturday, while going through her ordeal, she sat in the hospital exhausted and depressed. It seemed as if her first born child was not getting better. She moaned in her heart, "Jesus!" A church member visiting the hospital was passing by her daughter's room, recognized her and went in.

She spoke to the daughter first, then to my friend. These were the words my friend remembered that kindled her faith, "Sister, if you have faith as small as a mustard seed, your daughter can be healed!"

When the lady left the room my friend began to pray to the Most High God. She asked God to let this be the last night her daughter spends in the hospital bed. A

This shows us that not everything which comes our way or upon us, we must succumb to it. We can rise up, declare in the Name of Jesus and say to whatever circumstance, be removed and it shall be done. This may sound like a hard thing but it takes faith. Jesus once said "If we have faith as small as a mustard seed we can say to the mountain move from one place to another and it shall be done." -Matthew: 17:20.

few days later, they were released. As she told this story to me she cried, remembering what Jesus had done for her. God is an awesome God. Her daughter is now ten years old and has never suffered an asthma attack. Praise be to God!

Chapter 6   A Stove for Christmas

From 2014 to 2015, my friend prepared her family's meals with a stove that had a damaged oven and burners that smoked which caused a mess of her cookware. As the Christmas season approached my friend prayerfully sought God for the financial assistance to purchase a stove. Time drew closer and she concluded that it would be financially impossible. One evening, a sister in Christ told her that a store in one of the neighboring US Virgin Islands had a sale on stoves. She became elated and informed her husband. They went online, saw the stoves that were available and chose the one that they liked. The next day she asked her employer for permission to have it shipped on one of their chartered fleets. He agreed!

Jesus knows our need, whether it is considered to be significant or insignificant. He is a God who hears us when we earnestly seek Him.

That same week her employer suddenly had to leave for another Caribbean Island on business. This caused everything to be at a standstill until he returned. The word of God is truth, Isaiah 65:24 says "And it shall come to pass, that before they call, I will answer; and while they are yet speaking, I will hear." Hallelujah to the Lamb! When her employer came back it was only a few days before Christmas. She still didn't have the stove. Seeing that it was too late to order the stove from the neighboring US Island her employer surprised her with a blank check to go and get herself a stove. She was not expecting this. What a blessing! A new stove for Christmas.

Chapter 7   Instant Obedience

I heard my name. I was nineteen and living in Canada. The adults had left for work and the children had taken the bus to school. On these mornings when I was home alone, I would go out on the frozen pond and try to ice-skate or just take a walk in the crisp cold country air. However, on this particular day I did not do this, I stayed indoors. While walking past the main entrance, going towards the kitchen, I heard my name. I cannot say if I was scared but this much I do know, the way in which my name was spoken caught my attention. My name was never spoken like that before, as if it filled every volume of space in the area where I was.

I stopped immediately in my tracks with one foot forward and the other behind in my stride. The voice continued to speak, it said, "Go and lock the door." *The door was closed but not locked.* Instantly, I turned and went to the main entrance door and turned the deadbolt on the door. I turned to walk away from the door, and in my stride as before one foot forward

My friends each day as you awake, turn your life over to the Lord. Put your life in the Lord's hands. I did not know that the enemy was sending his forces to me in such a manner, but my Redeemer knew. He also protected me, by using me. Had I not obeyed my Master's voice instantly, I would not have liked to envision that outcome. John 10:27 says, "My sheep hear my voice, and I know them and they follow me." "For the Lord will not cast off his people neither will he forsake his inheritance." -Psalm 94:14

and one behind, there was a loud shaking of the heavy wooden door. Someone was trying to get in. The person would have been close enough to have heard when the lock snapped closed.

Nothing was said, I was just shaking. I was scared with what was happening and also when I realized what could have happened. I ran and went under my bed. I cried and cried, I prayed and prayed. I knew without a shadow of a doubt that the Lord had just saved me.

There was a broken basement door on the other side of the house and that caused me to be afraid. I prayed and prayed. Eventually, the person left. The would-be intruder that caused my angel or my Jesus to call me by my name was evidently stopped in his tracks from getting any closer to me. I knew that day Jesus saved my life, but I figured my life was also spared because I instantly obeyed.

Chapter 8   Small Blessings

On one particular night, I only had twelve dollars for gas for my jeep. I decided to ask the Lord to stretch my twelve dollars because it was all I had. I drove up to the attendant at the gas station, said goodnight, and proceeded to tell him I needed twelve dollars gas. He then pumped the gas and I paid him. On paying him, He said, "Oh it was twelve dollars you needed, I thought you said twenty!"

"Oh," I responded, "but I said twelve dollars".

"But my God shall supply all your needs according to His riches in glory by Christ Jesus." -Philippians 4:19. Even in such things, the Lord cares and He supplies.

"Don't bother about it," He replied.

So for the good deed that was done, I asked him his name and bade him a good night. As I the left the gas station that night, I thanked the Lord for the blessing of the extra fuel.

Chapter 9   New Fridge

For quite some time the fridge I had was not working properly. Experts would come in and check it but it would work for a while then stop. I even anointed my fridge. I needed a new fridge. The old one looked so embarrassing. I began talking to the Lord about getting a new fridge at a rate that I'll be able to pay. I could not go to the department store because I did not have the cash to pay for it. Then the Lord answered my prayer.

The Lord cares about our livelihood. He cares about us and He loves us. Friends we are to trust God. Isaiah 65:24 says, "Before they call I will answer and while they are yet speaking, I will bring it to pass." Try Him today.

A brother at the church I attend had an empty apartment with a new fridge that was just purchased a couple months before. He heard me talking about my fridge and offered to sell it to me for whatever price I could afford. I was astonished and overjoyed. The gentleman did not name a payment for me, he actually said what I could afford. God had answered my prayer. My new fridge even came with a surge protector that I did not have to pay for. My fridge is an enhancement to my kitchen and to my faith.

Chapter 10 Scheduled for Surgery

I was in my early stages of pregnancy when I discovered a lump in my breast. A lump that seemed as if it was attached by a root in my breast. What was this, at this time in my life? Whatever was about to happen, my baby was going to live. As the days passed by I contemplated what was going on. I did not even remember mentioning this to my gynecologist. One day while visiting my parent's home, I decided to take a walk through their garden. As I was walking my thoughts went to this lump that was growing in my breast and while meditating the

Lord brought Romans 4:3 to me, where Abraham believed God and it was counted to him for righteousness. I knew that I must have faith and trust God with what I was about to face. I decided I must have faith. I must have faith.

As my baby grew the lump grew, there was no denying it. At this point, I mentioned it to my gynecologist who decided we could not deal with it for the sake of the child until I gave birth. I put the lump to the back of my mind and put my faith in God as my source of strength. I enjoyed my

My dear friend, the same God who did this for me can do the same and anything for you. You must trust Him. Jeremiah 17:14 says "Heal me O Lord, and I shall be healed, save me and I shall be saved; for thou art my praise." You may not be a worshipper, you may not be someone who praises Him, but if you can earnestly believe He can do what he says He can, He can help you in whatever situation you are in. He is God.

pregnancy as much as I could and truly had faith in God where this was concerned.

After giving birth, I decided I was going to breastfeed my child until the recommended months for weaning, which I did through faith in God.

The time came when I had to deal with the lump that had grown into a mass, almost the size of a grapefruit. There were times when I was afraid and times when my faith was absolutely strong. I prayed every day since the beginning of my pregnancy for God to heal me from the lump in my breast. I believed that he could do it. I visited specialists who guided me through the process as well. Some tests were done and I was scheduled for surgery. I cried and prayed to the Lord continually, night and day for healing. Before my surgery was done, the hospital's policy was that the head surgeon must look over a patient's file and give the consent to proceed.

In my case, however, he did not give permission to continue. He said he would like to perform some more tests and seeing that I had a history of fibrocystic problems, he felt that I may not have to do the surgery. The mass had increased but was benign. What a relief to know it was benign. I praised God for that miracle. The surgeon prescribed some medication for me which he thought could reduce the size of the mass. However, to me, I did not see or feel any reduction in the size of the mass. I kept praying that the Lord would heal me from this thing in my breast.

One morning when I awoke and got out of bed, I checked my breast and it was gone. No mass, no lump. I checked both breasts and they were free of mass or any lumps at all. I praised God. I praised Him and I could not believe He had done it. He had done it, He had healed me. I had the faith, I trusted Him, and He came through. I love this God that I serve.

Chapter 11 Ask of Him
          What Ye Will

Throughout her years my daughter has been an A student. The Lord has blessed her in this area. When she was about one year and some months, not quite two years of age, she did something that made me think this child has been blessed. One night while tucking her into bed, I asked her to say the Lord's Prayer. She began with, Our Father, who art in Heaven and continued throughout the whole prayer without any mistakes at all. I was amazed, I could not believe what this child had just done. You see, from the time she was in the womb I read to her and prayed for her. After she was born, each night I would say those prayers for her as I tucked her into bed. That night when I asked her to say the prayer for herself, I did not expect too much. However, she blew my mind.

After that day, she was nicknamed Cum Laude, which my husband and I pronounced with a 'y' instead of the 'e'. Throughout her childhood, I

Even the little ones can believe God can do anything for them. "If ye shall ask what ye will, it shall be done unto you." -John 15:7 We serve an Awesome God!

would pray for her as her mother. I would pray for her spirituality, her grades, her health, her humility and anything you can think of that a mother can pray for her child. As she grew, she had her challenges but the Lord kept her.

In her final year of elementary school, she wanted to be the valedictorian of her class. Children do have dreams of their own. One day she came home from school in tears, an adult had told her that she could not be the valedictorian, no not her. I used that moment to pray for my daughter and encouraged her that she can be anything that she wanted to be with the help of the Lord. We prayed for this and other things concerning her and we continued to pray while she prepared for these exams. As her mother, I prayed and fasted for her.

The day came for final exams. This day we prayed for her that God will give her wisdom and understanding as she did her exams. When the results came out, my daughter was not only the valedictorian in her class but she was also first in the territory. The exams that were done for the elementary schools were nationwide. To God be the Glory. I continue to pray for my daughter each day that she will know the Lord for herself so that when He comes to take his people home, he will find her faithful.

Chapter 12   Sting Ray

One of the most enjoyable things to do in the Caribbean is sailing. We were on one of our sailing trips that lasted for six days with two other families. We boarded the yacht on Friday, anchored for Sabbath so we could attend church, then set sail on Sunday to enjoy the few days off. Yes, sailing to the different Islands was fantastic. The nights were most enjoyable, under the night skies, in an anchorage where the water was calm.

On this particular day we had sail to one of the islands in the archipelago. The children wanted to swim after lunch so we anchored and took the dingy to shore. While the children were swimming along the shore having fun, two fishermen were cleaning fish on the jetty. This caused that area to attract different types of fish. I was swimming close to the shore and

We have an awesome God. Get to know Jesus. When you can hear a caution, or a whisper from Him, it is truly a great thing. God's promises are great. "The Lord will give grace and glory, no good thing will He withhold from them that walk uprightly." -Psalm 84:11.

decided to take a rest right on the shore line where the waves were breaking.

While resting, I was looking at the children as they were swimming and playing. They were enjoying themselves. Just then, I thought I heard something. The waves were gently slapping the shore, but it wasn't that, it was a rhythmic sound. Something told me to stand up. I stood up, and directly swimming towards me approximately nine feet away, was a big, broad, black stingray. My heart jolted. I ran and screamed for the children to get out of the water. The stingray then turned towards the direction of the children. They ran to safety and it stayed for a while then left. I thank God for sparing us from that stingray.